OUR WORLD IN COLOUR

DELHI, AGRA & JAIPUR

OUR WORLD IN COLOUR
DELHI, AGRA & JAIPUR

Photography by Steve Vidler
Text by Louise Nicholson
Captions by Shobita Punja and Bikram Grewal
A-Z by Jasbir Singh

The Guidebook Company Limited

Title spread
*Edward Lear, the poet, wrote of
the Taj Mahal 'the inhabitants
of the world are divided into
them as has seen the Taj Mahal
and them that hasn't'. This
great mausoleum was built in
the 17th century by Shah Jahan
in memory of his wife
Mumtaz Mahal.*

Right
*One of the vast gateways along
the two-kilometre (1.2-mile)
-long walls of the Purana Qila
is reflected in the surrounding
moat. The Purana Qila, which
lies in east Delhi, was
successively enlarged by several
emperors including Humayun
and Sher Shah Sur.*

Pages 6-7
*The sun sets over the
Secretariat complex. Built by
Herbert Baker and situated next
to the old viceregal palace, it
houses several administrative
offices including that of the
Prime Minister and the Army
Headquarters. It also forms the
backdrop to the Beating Retreat
ceremony in late January.*

Pages 8-9
*Marble relief panel from the Taj
Mahal. Both the artist and
sculptor strove to idealize the
flowers, capturing the natural
twist of the leaf and curl of the
petal. The marble flowers reflect
those that once grew in the
organized gardens around the
tomb of Mumtaz Mahal.*

Pages 10-11
*Built on a natural outcrop of
the Aravali hills to the north of
Jaipur, the fortified palace of
Amber was constructed by Man
Singh I and Jai Singh I in the
early 17th century. The
rambling exterior belies the
well-organized bejewelled
interior of palaces, gardens and
courtyards.*

Photography by Steve Vidler
Front cover by Fredrik Arvidsson
Text by Louise Nicholson
Captions by Shobita Punja and Bikram Grewal
A-Z by Jasbir Singh

Edited by Nick Wallwork
Series Editor: Caroline Robertson
Original designed by Joan Law Design & Photography
Artwork by Aubrey Tse, Au Yeung Chui Kwai
Created by Gulmohur Press, New Delhi
Production House: Twin Age Ltd, Hong Kong

Printed in Hong Kong

ISBN 962-217-123-0

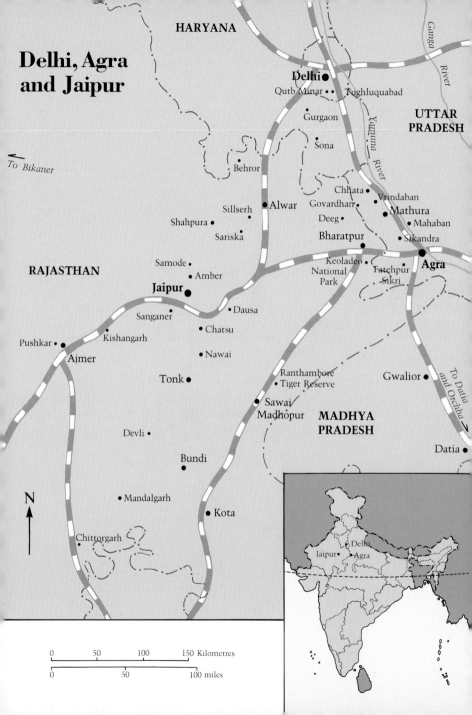

INTRODUCTION

DELHI, AGRA AND JAIPUR, with their teeming life and proud monuments, all give a glimpse into the rich culture of India, past and present. New Delhi, capital of the world's largest democracy, is the last and most elegant of a string of capitals built on this site by successive masters of northern India. Agra, which enjoyed a century-and-a-half of unimaginable splendour under the great Mughal emperors, still nurtures craftsmen descended from those who chiselled marble into life for the Taj Mahal. Jaipur, the pink-painted city built by an enlightened maharaja, retains all the romance of fairy-tale palaces, legendary valour, and bejewelled beauties bargaining in colourful bazaars.

To visit all three cities is to taste something of the vast range of experiences India has to offer. Each has its own character, traditions and culture. And while the origins of each are lost in the mists of myth, there are moments in history when their stories interweave.

Delhi

The gods founded Delhi, and it has been an irresistible capital for humans since records began. The great Hindu myth, the *Mahabharata* — at 90,000 stanzas the world's longest poem — tells the story. Five Pandava brother heroes founded Indraprastha as the capital of their kingdom, Hastinapura, beside the River Yamuna in the first millennium BC. (Archaeologists' finds did indeed include pottery, suggesting that a township flourished around that time.)

Here at Indraprastha — named after Indra, the god of rain and thunder — the brothers lived in a splendid palace until the eldest foolishly gambled away his kingdom, his brothers and their shared wife, Draupadi, in a game of dice. Finally, after 13 years in exile and a great war, he won them all back, and the brothers ruled in peace for many years. Eventually they set out for the Himalayas where they climbed Mount Meru and entered paradise.

In reality, it was Delhi's strategic position that made it the key to power — and riches — in the subcontinent. It lay on the banks of the life-giving Yamuna, a tributary of the great mother Ganga River. Here, on the flat fertile plain, almost every triumphant conqueror would lay waste the defeated city and build a fresh one, often naming it after himself. The site has had eight major cities (plus many smaller strongholds), energetic bursts of building by powerful rulers anxious to be remembered by posterity. Yet only two of the cities still live.

The Delhis begin with Dilli, the Tomar Rajputs' stronghold in the eighth to tenth centuries. Their oblong citadel of Lal Kot was so sturdily built that its robust ramparts not only provided the nucleus of the first official Delhi but still stand today. The next rulers were the Chauhan Rajputs, whose hero-king Prithviraj III built Qila Rai Pithora and named it after himself. During Chauhan rule, the wonderful iron pillar was set up. Its Sanskrit inscription records that it was, as a standard of the god Vishnu, made in memory of the Gupta king, Chandragupta II, and a hole at the top suggests that Vishnu's mythical sunbird, Garuda, sat on top. But how those fourth-century workmen fashioned the almost pure malleable iron is still a mystery.

In 1192, Prithviraj lost his city to the Turkish invader Qutb-ud-din Aibak, who proclaimed himself sultan in 1206. Thus Hindu rule ended and Muslim rule began. During the Delhi Sultanate (1206–1526), the Slave, Khalji, Tughluq, Sayyid and Lodi sultans took their turns, and under their rule the Muslim and Hindu cultures fused to create a rich Indo-Islamic society. After the Sultanate, Muslim rule continued under the Mughals until 1858, when the last emperor was bundled off to Burma by the British, and the Indians had to look across the seas to Queen-Empress Victoria.

Qutb-ud-din Aibak, the first Slave sultan, merely added to the exisiting Delhi, employing local Hindus to tear down temples and re-use the stones for India's first

For a rupee one can get a shave, haircut, massage, have one's ears cleaned, nails trimmed and exchange local gossip.

In recent years there has been an encouraging increase in domestic tourism, partially due to the rise in personal incomes and benefits of an extensive school system.

mosque, the Quwwat-ul-Islam Masjid (Might of Islam Mosque). He also gave Delhi one of its best-known landmarks, the Qutb Minar, an intricately carved tower that served as both muezzin's minaret to call the faithful to prayer and a symbol of justice, sovereignty and Islam. In 1831, while the Mughal emperor was visiting, a madman ran up to the top, laughed at everyone below and jumped off. As an amazed traveller reported, 'he kept his erect position till about half-way down, when he turned over, and continued to turn until he got to the bottom, when his fall made a report like a gun. He was of course dashed to pieces.' Today, the tower is closed.

Later sultans built four fresh cities whose remains, with those of the earlier ones, lie at peace in the scrubland south of modern Delhi. Ala-ud-din Khalji, perhaps the ablest sultan of all, built Siri in about 1303. It was a grand place with seven gates, many mosques, markets which were inspected daily to check that prices were fair, and running water supplied from a huge reservoir. The three Delhis of the Tughluq sultans followed. Tughluqabad was first built by Ghiyas-ud-din in the 1320s. You can clamber up steps and through mighty ramparts into the octagonal, 13-gate fort and roam the romantic remains of soaring arches, colonnades, palaces and citadel. Ghiyas-ud-din's son, the mad genius Muhammad, committed patricide in 1325 and then laid out the fresh city of Jahanpanah, near Siri, before marching his citizens some 1,500 kilometres south to a new capital at Daulatabad, only to march them back again a few years later.

But it was Feroz Shah, Ghiyas-ud-din's nephew, who laid out the most impressive Tughluq city. In its heyday the palaces, mosques, hunting lodges, reservoirs, hospitals and colleges sprawled over a huge area and buzzed with scholarly and artistic life; the surviving Feroz Shah Kotla was merely its riverside citadel. And it was Feroz Shah, intellectual and antiquarian, who placed one of the remarkable Ashoka pillars here, bringing it by boat down the Yamuna. He thought it was a magic charm used in religious ritual; in fact it bears the Brahmi script message of Ashoka, the great Mauryan emperor of the third century BC, and promotes *dharma* (the Buddhist teachings) and the welfare and happiness of the people.

Tragedy struck Feroz Shah's dreamy world in 1398. Timur, also known as Tamburlaine, sacked the city, carrying off as loot not only its much-prized elephants and stonemasons but so much gold, jewels and other wealth that 'they could scarcely march four miles a day'. Such marauding was to suck the wealth no less than four times from a later Delhi, the one built, ironically, by Timur's distant descendant, Shah Jahan.

But before that great city came one more. The ramparts of Purana Qila soar up between Delhi's zoo — which gives refuge to rare Asiatic lions, the Assamese one-horned rhinoceros and dazzling, brightly-feathered birds — and the Crafts Museum, a microcosm of the range of skills still practised all over India today. The fort's first occupants were, it is believed, the Pandavas, for this is perhaps the site of Indraprastha. Later, Humayun, the second Mughal emperor, moved the capital back from Agra, where it had been established by Babur. Full of optimism, he founded Dinpanah (Shelter of the Faith) in 1533, dreaming of a cultural capital to rival Samarkand. His are the great walls and gateways. But Humayun was no politician or general. By 1540 the talented Afghan, Sher Shah Sur, was sitting in his place. He extended the city and introduced an administrative system which was taken up by Humayun's son, the great emperor Akbar, to consolidate Mughal power. In 1556, having won back his city, Humayun fell to his death down the steps of Sher Mandal, which he had made his library. But his widow, Bega Begum, ensured his name would be remembered: looking south across the valley that contains Delhi zoo, you can glimpse Humayun's tomb, the first great Mughal garden tomb, built to a design which reached mature perfection in the Taj Mahal at Agra.

After these ghost cities, peopled only by the imagination, Delhi's final two cities seethe with life today. In the maze of lanes in Old Delhi you can find cloth, oil, grain and spice markets operating just as they did when this was a city to rival London and Paris. Behind one dark façade, a blindfolded bullock plods round in circles to extract almond oil; behind another, a craftsman descended from those who served the Mughal courtiers works precious gold into delicate filigree; and in the spice bazaar behind Fatehpuri Mosque, fat merchants weigh out piles of glowing red chillies on huge scales. At the Jama Masjid (Friday Mosque), the faithful file up the steep steps to answer the muezzin's call to prayer, while in the surrounding bazaars merchants squat in their box-like shops stocked floor to ceiling with sweet perfumes, exotic wedding saris, fireworks, gold braid, glittering jewellery and crazy, colourful masks for Hindu festivals. If you are lucky, you may glimpse a bridegroom, decked out in gold turban, riding a decorated horse up the main street, Chandni Chowk, and preceded by trumpeters and drummers.

This is the thriving city founded by Shah Jahan. Not content with the marble palaces he added at Agra, or with the Taj Mahal, a mausoleum to his beloved wife, he threw himself into the largest and most successful town-planning project of any of the great Mughal emperors; though they were all great builders, as borne out by cities from Humayun's Dinpanah to Akbar's Fatehpur Sikri, those cities are now dead, while Shah Jahan's still pulsates round the clock.

It was in 1648 that Shah Jahan entered his new city, bringing the capital back from Agra to irresistible Delhi, which had been forsaken by the Lodi sultans in 1504. Following tradition, he called it Shahjahanabad. The great riverside fort contained palaces, bazaars, gardens, and halls of audience; the walled city outside it bustled with every kind of merchant serving the thousands of courtiers, diplomats, soldiers and hangers-on. Inside Lal Qila (Red Fort), glittering with inlaid precious stones, gold ceilings and silk rugs, he set up the vast empire's administrative headquarters, spent freely from his coffers stuffed with gold and jewels, sat on his gem-encrusted Peacock Throne to hold court and, apparently, said 'If on earth there be a paradise of bliss, It is this, it is this, it is this.' The gems and gold have gone, but the perfectly proportioned buildings remain.

Nine years later, Shah Jahan's blissful Delhi life ended when his son imprisoned him and usurped the throne. Mughal splendour ended; during the long reign of Aurangzeb its deterioration began. The increasingly powerful British at last won Delhi in 1803; but they permitted the now powerless puppet emperors to play out their last years until, following the 1857 War of Independence (also known as the Mutiny), the British won back Delhi. The last emperor, Bahadur Shah II, was deposed in 1858 and was deported to Burma where he died four years later.

The custom of women covering their heads is predominant in northern and western India as a direct result of Islamic influence.

By now Delhi was no more than a strategic backwater. Calcutta was the British capital. But, for one final time, Delhi proved irresistible. At the grand Delhi Durbar of 1911, the King-Emperor George V announced that the capital of the eastern empire would move from Calcutta back to the traditional political seat of power in India, Delhi. Sir Edwin Lutyens, helped by Sir Herbert Baker, laid out a new city, the most perfect planned city built this century.

It was an optimistic act. Inaugurated in 1931, this stunning 'Anglo-Indian Rome' became the capital of independent India just 16 years later. Today, New Delhi, with its wide tree-lined avenues, its flower-filled parks and its elegant buildings, is the political nerve-centre of India. At Rastrapati Bhavan, the President entertains state guests; in the circular Lok Sabha, politicians debate with passion the problems of their new country; and at Connaught Circus — a sort of colonial Cheltenham — locals shop for everything from traditional silk saris to air-cooling fans. The homes of India's first Prime Minister, Jawaharlal Nehru, and his daughter, Indira Gandhi, are both museums, as is the house where Indian's greatest freedom fighter, Mahatma Gandhi, was assassinated. And on Republic Day (26 January) the grand parades up Raj Path are relayed on television to the 900 million Indians of the subcontinent.

India is the world's largest producer of scooters.

The Agra Fort was built by the great Mughal Emperor Akbar, whose architecture is dominated by the use of red sandstone. His grandson Shah Jahan, builder of the Taj Mahal, later added palaces built in his favoured marble within the fort.

Agra

Agra, too, has its roots in ancient Hindu myths, which called it Agrabana, meaning paradise. Much later, in the 16th century, when the Mughal conquerors chose Agra as the capital of their vast empire, their sumptuous extravagance, blended with exquisite taste in all the arts, made Agra an utterly luxurious paradise on earth.

Theirs was a court where a favourite fish might be fitted with a gold nose-ring, where a queen discovered how to capture and distil the heavy scent of rose petals, where a prince's dress was decorated with pearls and where a single giant ruby was fashioned into a ring. It was a court where twice a year the emperor was weighed in gold and silver which was then distributed to his people. As for food, even humble rice was coloured gold and eaten with gossamer-thin sheets of real gold and silver. Chefs were given the title 'maharaj', meaning great king.

In short, it was a fairy-tale court whose dazzling rays stretched as far as Europe. Envoys hurried eastwards to verify the fabled 'gold of Ind'. Ralph Fitch, arriving in 1584, was one of the first English merchants to come in search of trade; Sir Thomas Roe, who came in 1615, was England's first ambassador, sent by James I. Travellers' diaries became bestsellers; accounts included those by Peter Mundy, who watched the Taj Mahal being built; and Niccolao Manucci, an Italian quack-doctor, who spiced up his observations with juicy gossip. Traders were quick to take advantage of India's wealth. One of them, a French jewel-merchant named Jean-Baptiste Tavernier, came five times and bought gems to take home and also sold some to the Emperor Aurangzeb.

But why Agra, when Delhi had been the stronghold for past conquerors? The new town at Agra on the banks of the Yamuna some 195 kilometres (122 miles) south of Delhi, was founded in 1504 by Sikandar, the Lodi sultan of Delhi, in order to control his provincial chiefs more effectively by being nearer them.

Twenty-two years later Babur arrived. A Turk of the Burlas tribe, he was poet, diarist, soldier, statesman and adventurer rolled into one. Among his forbears were two soldier heroes: Timur (Tamburlaine) and Genghis Khan. In 1526, on his fifth raid into the subcontinent, he defeated Sikandar's successor, Ibrahim, at the Battle of Panipat. The following year he triumphed over a confederacy of fierce Rajput rulers at the Battle of Khanua.

Babur was the first of the six great Mughal emperors who, father to son, consolidated and expanded the empire and brought it to unimaginable heights of splendour.

Babur made Agra his capital, and laid out the first of many Mughal gardens there. The now rather wild garden still retains a royal atmosphere of the days when he received delegations from local chieftains. Humayun, his son, returned to Delhi. Agra really began to shine under Akbar, his grandson, who combined soldiering with religious tolerance and marriage alliances, and who set the tone for Mughal patronage of the arts, from building to painting to music-making.

It was Akbar who built the magnificent riverside fort with its sturdy double walls. Outside lived the citizens, in the narrow lanes that are still vibrant with life today. Here you can seek out craftsmen descended from those who embroidered velvet for the Mughal courtiers, inlaid marble buildings with precious stones, and wove rugs and dhurries. And it was Akbar who, in 1571, aged just 29 but already emperor for 15 years, built his ideal city, Fatehpur Sikri, in thanks for the birth of his sons. Though Agra remained the military stronghold it was this personal dream palace-city that became the artistic and intellectual centre. Just as suddenly, it was abandoned in 1585, to become the world's most perfect ghost-city, its red sandstone palace buildings as crisp as when they were chiselled, and the silent air around it no longer echoing with the sounds of court life, dancing, debate, music and the emperor's daily meetings with his people.

But Agra fort was not abandoned. As each emperor reaped greater riches from his empire, so new buildings were increasingly grand. Akbar had built in red sandstone; Jahangir, whose name means Seizer of the World, inlaid it with marble for his new palace façade. Then came Shah Jahan, whose name means Ruler of the World, and who was the most lavish builder of them all. He added the string of marble palaces along the river front, using only the finest building material: pure white, gleaming marble. And for decoration, he again ordered only the best: *pietra dura* inlay of delicate floral arabesques composed of precious and semi-precious stones. The most delicate work of all is in the Mussaman Burj, a mini-palace intended for his beloved wife, Mumtaz Mahal, with courtyard, baths, living room and breeze-catching terrace.

But tragedy struck. This beautiful woman, who had been adviser and companion to Shah Jahan on all his military campaigns for 17 years, died in 1631 giving birth to their 14th child. Shah Jahan was heartbroken. He mourned for two years, then threw himself into building. First he built the tomb for his wife, the Taj Mahal, the perfect Mughal garden tomb. Completed some 22 years later, it was described as 'a most perfect pearl on an azure ground' by the painter William Hodges. Perhaps its most sublime moment is at dawn, when it seems to rouse itself from slumber as the sun's rays catch the top of the dome and then slide down the marble to give it life for another hot day. Shah Jahan then returned the capital to Delhi, building a whole new city, Shahjahanabad. But just before he left Agra, he added the sublime Moti Masjid, or Pearl Mosque. The emperor's life ended with more tragedy: his son, Aurangzeb, deposed him and kept him prisoner here at Agra, in the Mussaman Burj. For the last eight years of his life, Shah Jahan could only gaze across the bend in the Yamuna River to his wife's tomb, the Taj Mahal, the greatest monument to love. After his death in 1666 he was buried beside her. Even today, this view of the Taj has a romantic poignancy, particularly when it glows under an afternoon sun.

There are two other great tombs at Agra. Akbar's great mausoleum on the outskirts of Sikandra is set in a lush park which was the site of the Lodi fort; a few Lodi remains are sprinkled about. The other belongs to Itimad-ud-Daulah, the head of an ambitious family that in time became a powerful extension of no less than the royal family. Itimad-ud-Daulah, meaning Pillar of the Government, was the title of this Persian adventurer who rose to become chief minister to Emperor Jahangir. His beautiful daughter married the emperor — it is said they met at a fair in the fort — and became known as Nur Jahan, meaning Light of the World. Asaf Khan, Nur Jahan's brother, became deputy chief minister, and his daughter continued family fortunes by marrying Shah Jahan and taking the name Mumtaz Mahal, meaning Chosen One of the Palace. Itimad's tomb, built by Nur Jahan, lies on the far bank of the Yamuna. It stands in its garden like a delicate casket, inlaid with coloured stones on the outside and coated with richly-coloured murals inside.

Thus it was that the most beautiful of Agra's monuments were dedicated to two members of an adventurer's family, and not to Mughal emperors: the Taj for Mumtaz and the tomb for her grandfather.

Fatehpur Sikri, built by the Emperor Akbar (top). Mughal palaces here were constructed to contend with the extreme heat of the region. Water from rivers and fountains helped cool the rooms during the hot summers.

Agra's grand Mughal monuments are surrounded by an area which was built as the British cantonment. After Shah Jahan went to Delhi in 1648, Agra lay in quietness until the British, who had established their power in India as traders under the East India Company, made it the capital of Agra (later the North-Western) Province in 1830. As elsewhere, the British laid out an ordered camp, or cantonment, on the edge of the existing Agra. Rarely for India, Agra's cantonment has retained its spaciousness. You can easily imagine the carriages spinning along The Mall, past memsahibs sitting in deep, shaded verandahs or clipping the bougainvillea and roses in their gardens. In this toytown evocation of 'Home', Queen Mary's Library still stands, as does St George's Church, where Raj families dressed in their Sunday best would attend matins and then buy jam at the church fête.

Jaipur

The gods also had a hand in Jaipur's beginnings. The city was the later capital of the Kachchwaha clan of Rajputs, who first arrived in the 12th century at the old fort-palace of Amber up in the protective Aravalli hills, a few miles away. The Kachchwaha belonged to the Kshatriya, or the warrior caste of Hindus, but they traced their origins back to the sun, via Kusa who was the twin son of the god Rama.

The people the Kachchwahas ousted at Amber were the Susawat Minas, who became the hereditary and loyal guards of what would turn into one of the largest and most valuable treasuries in India. For, from this well-protected base, the Kachchwaha Rajputs, with their brilliant soldiering, coupled with a canny eye for lucrative alliances (even if that meant swallowing Rajput pride), amassed a fortune. Above all, it was the special relationship the Amber rulers developed with the Mughals that brought them real power, influence and wealth.

Arriving from Jaipur through the narrow pass in the hills, you are presented with a view of the honey-coloured Amber fort-palace that conforms to every expectation of how a romantic Rajput fort should appear. It rambles over a rugged hill, reflected in Maota Lake below. The odd elephant plods up the ramparts road. In Amber village, which clusters around the hill, gem-cutters patiently smooth and cut stones, the faithful go to mosques and temples, and children run around the royal *chhatris* (mausoleums) and in and out of decaying painted houses. A circle of protective hills surrounds all this, and snaking up these hills are crenellated walls punctuated by look-out posts. On the highest ridge and overlooking the whole valley sits Jaigarh Fort. It is a spectacular display of powerful defence. Inside Amber Fort, the contrast is sharp: the grand painted gateway, the hall of public audience that made even the Mughal emperor jealous, pools and cascades to cool the air in summer heat, and the hall of mirrors inlaid with tiny pieces of glass so that a single flame creates a room of a thousand stars — all is refined, glittering and bejewelled.

The power to create such a strong fort enclosing such beauty was built up over several generations. Raja Bihar Mal made the first move. Recognizing Mughal power, he paid homage to the emperor Humayun and led a 5,000-strong army for him. Then he made sure he was the first Rajput presented at Akbar's court. His big chance came when Akbar made his first annual pilgrimage to Ajmer, the burial place of a Muslim saint, which lay in Kachchwaha territory. On a visit to Akbar's tent, Bihar Mal gave his daughter to be the emperor's wife and his adopted grandson, Man Singh, into royal service. The daughter finally gave Akbar his first son, who became emperor Jahangir. The next ruler, Bhagwan Das, cemented the alliance and gave a daughter to be Jahangir's wife.

Then came the two rulers who built Amber: Man Singh, a leading general under both Akbar and Jahangir, and Jai Singh I, a military and diplomatic genius who brought the house of Amber to its apogee at the Mughal court. On the throne aged 11, Jai Singh I was soon commanding a Mughal force for Jahangir, then fought all over the Mughal empire for Shah Jahan and finally backed the right side in the war for succession and became emperor Aurangzeb's most prized Rajput commander.

All this time, the Kachchwaha coffers were filling with prizes, rewards and booty. And it continued. Three rulers later, Jai Singh II, another child prodigy, came to the throne. The young lad quickly impressed the 71-year-old Aurangzeb who awarded him the title 'Sawai', meaning one-and-a-quarter. Even today, the flag flying above the City Palace in Jaipur has an extra, quarter-sized one next to it, reminding fellow Rajputs of Jaipur superiority. For Jai Singh II, having proved his Rajput soldiering ability and further enriched his coffers, fulfilled his other passions — the arts and sciences. Confident of peace and stability, he abandoned the rugged hills of Amber and laid out a perfect, humanist palace-city down on the plains. In 1727, he laid the foundation stone of his dream city, aided by a remarkable architect, Vidyadhar Bhat-

Hawa Mahal, or Palace of the Winds, (top) in Jaipur was built in 1799 by Maharaja Pratap Singh. The Jantar Mantar (centre), also in Jaipur, is an open-air observatory built in 1728 by Jai Singh II.

tacharaya. And he called it Jaipur, a double-edged self-compliment as 'Jai' referred both to himself and also means victory. Certainly, it lived up to its name, for after Indian independence it was this city which became the vibrant capital of Rajasthan, the state constituted by a consolidation of the Rajput principalities.

Vidyadhar used a grid pattern of seven blocks of buildings divided by very wide, tree-lined avenues, with the palace set on the north side. Surrounding it are high walls pierced by ten gates which were firmly closed at night until recently. Jai Singh II added his ideas of hygiene, beauty and commerce; merchants and craftsmen from other cities were invited to come and live in specially allotted areas. It was the first sizable city in north India to be built from scratch to a single plan. But the famous pink colour symbolizing welcome came later, when Ram Singh II spruced up the whole city for the Prince of Wales's visit in 1876.

Today, Jaipur is much as it was when first built, and is still a bustling trading centre. Take, for example, Badi Chaupar crossroads. At one corner, gaggles of girls wrapped in brightly-coloured saris chatter and giggle as they drool at walls of delicate, multi-coloured bangles. Rising high above them is the Hawa Mahal, the five-storey, pyramid-shaped grand stand for the women of the palace to see (without being seen) all the street parades and processions. In another corner, in front of the silver shops, a family buys freshly threaded garlands of flowers. In another, a handsome local with blood-red turban inspects a sackful of ginger. Puppet-sellers fight for pavement space with shoe-sellers, while down a nearby lane women nimbly tie tiny knots into yard upon yard of cloth which is then dyed crimson, orange or turquoise blue to make *bandhani* (tie-and-dye). In the road, snooty camels compete with scooter-rickshaws, bicycle-rickshaws, wobbly Tempo taxis filled with laughing schoolchildren, cars, buses and lorries — all delivering their loads amid ceaseless shrieks, shouts, hoots and honks. The air is never silent in Jaipur.

Again, take the City Palace. This is no silent empty palace. There is constant movement in Jalebi Chowk, the main square. The faithful scuttle out at one end to the favourite Jaipur temple, Govind Devi, to worship Govinda, the name for Krishna when he was a young cowherd flirting with the cowgirls. The other archway out of Jalebi Chowk leads round to the palace proper. Outside the main gateway stands Jai Singh II's extraordinary Jantar Mantar, an open-air observatory (he built others, too, including one at Delhi which was so successful that the Mughal court astrologers used it for their calculations). Through the gateway, the outer palace rooms are now a museum. Former royal chambers and courtyards house marble elephants, gold-embroidered clothes, extraordinarily fine arms and armour testifying to Kachchwaha valour, exquisite miniature paintings and bold floral carpets. The inner rooms, each one decorated with delicate murals, are the home of the former Maharaja of Jaipur, who is still very much the well-loved Maharaja to his people.

The Sheesh Mahal, or Hall of Mirrors, in the Amber Fort palace is ornamented by thousands of small mirrors that capture the sunlight during the day and shimmer at night with the reflection of a single lamp. The latticed windows overlook Maota Lake.

Following pages
The Secretariat buildings are illuminated to celebrate Republic Day on 26 January, Independence Day on 15 August, and Diwali — the Hindu festival of lights.

The British love of pomp and pageantry has been retained and is reflected in the spectacular uniforms and ceremonies (left and top) of the Indian army. Now called Rastrapati Bhavan and the residence of the President of India, the old viceregal palace (centre and above) forms an impressive backdrop for these occasions.

Right
The All India War Memorial Arch, better known as India Gate, was designed by Lutyens and completed in 1931. It commemorated the 60,000 British and Indian officers and soldiers who died in the Great War. More recently it has become a memorial to the unknown soldier.

The Republic Day parade, which takes place every year on 26 January, is watched by tens of thousands of enthusiastic viewers. Recent developments in technology have meant that two-thirds of India can now watch this spectacle on television. Informative tableaux from different states are the most popular with the children

India has a rich and ancient tradition of music, both folk and classical. Each region of India has its own form of specialized music and instruments. Republic Day provides an opportunity for musicians to come together and display their skills.

The fifth-century iron pillar (left), now in the courtyard of the mosque in the Qutb Minar complex, has puzzled scientists and historians for years because of its rust-free properties. The Qutb Minar complex (top and centre) is one of the earliest Islamic religious buildings in North India. The tower was built by Qutb-ud-din Aibak and his successor Iltutmish in the early 13th century. Old British imperial statues (above) from around both Delhi and New Delhi are now relegated to a 'graveyard' next to the site of the 1912 Durbar in North Delhi.

Right
The tomb of Safdarjang, Governor of Oudh, is the last example of the Mughal garden-tomb layout.

Built in memory of the second Mughal Emperor Humayun by his senior widow Bega Begum in 1565, this tomb is the first substantial example of Mughal tomb architecture. Its high arches and double dome are said to derive from Persian architecture. When fleeing the British in 1857, the last Mughal emperor, the poet Bahadur Shah Zafar, took shelter in this tomb but was captured and exiled to Rangoon where he died.

Above
Little girls in India are no different from those around the world in their love for fine clothes and jewellery.

Left
Built in the 15th century, the octagonal tomb of Muhammad Shah of the Sayyid Dynasty is found within the Lodi Gardens in South Delhi.

In 1655 the British explorer Terry remarked of India; 'the natives there show very much ingenuity in their curious manufactures, as in their silk stuffs which they most artificially weave, some very neatly mingled with silver or gold or both . . . they make likewise excellent carpets, cabinets, boxes, trunks, curiously wrought within and without, inlaid with elephants teeth or mother of pearl, ebony, tortoiseshell or wire.' This holds true equally for India today. Visitors would do well to explore the footpaths and smaller markets.

Despite its size, India has a remarkably well-developed postal system. Letters and money orders are delivered within a week to even the remotest villages. Unfortunately the same cannot be said about the efficiency of Delhi's public transport system (right).

The Gandhi Memorial Museum (top) houses a collection of photographs and other memorabilia of the Mahatma's life. The abstract shapes (above) are in fact of the observatory built in 1724 by Jai Singh II.

Right
The Lakshmi-Narayan Temple, more popularly known as the Birla Mandir, is a recent shrine built by a famous family of Indian industrialists. It is dedicated to Lord Vishnu and his consort Lakshmi, the goddess of wealth.

Left
Built in 1656, the Jama Masjid or the Friday Mosque was another of Shah Jahan's great creations. It is the largest mosque in India and on Fridays the 100-metre (yard) -square courtyard is filled with devotees.

Indian weddings are always elaborate. However, urban wealth often results in turning these occasions into a vulgar display of consumption. The entire community is involved in the elaborate celebrations.

Above and right
Finding the heat of Agra too oppressive and the streets too narrow, Shah Jahan shifted his capital to Delhi in 1638. Here on the banks of the Yamuna River he built a massive fort and laid the foundation of a brand-new city called Shahjahanabad. Lal Qila, or the Red Fort, was completed in 1648. The walls of the fort were made of red sandstone, hence the name.

Left
A Sunday market now takes place where the Yamuna River once flowed beside the Red Fort in Delhi.

The Purana Qila, or the Old Fort, occupies what is considered the site of the ancient city of Indraprastha, mentioned in the great Indian epic the Mahabharata. *It was built by Emperor Humayun and the Afghan ruler Sher Shah Sur in the early 16th century, and remains one of Delhi's most impressive monuments. Within the fort lies the Sher Mandal, a small octagonal tower used as a library by Emperor Humayun.*

Following the old Mughal road to Agra introduces the visitor to the glory of the Indian countryside. Villages dot the landscape and the sight of yellow mustard fields is unforgettable. The ancient 'mile' stones or kos minars *(left), which appear at intervals along the road, were built by Sher Shah Sur. A* kos *is the traditional way of measuring distances and is approximately three kilometres (two miles).*

Above
A traditional Rajasthani performer enacts the glorious deeds of his ancestors. Every region of India has its own form of roadside entertainment.

Right
A village snake-charmer entices his cobras from their baskets.

With its architectural simplicity, perfect balance and proportion of structure, the Taj Mahal is perhaps the most beautiful building in the world. The subtlety of the building, faced entirely with white marble, is enlivened by highlights of inlay and calligraphy in other coloured stones. The gentle white gives it a quality of weightlessness.

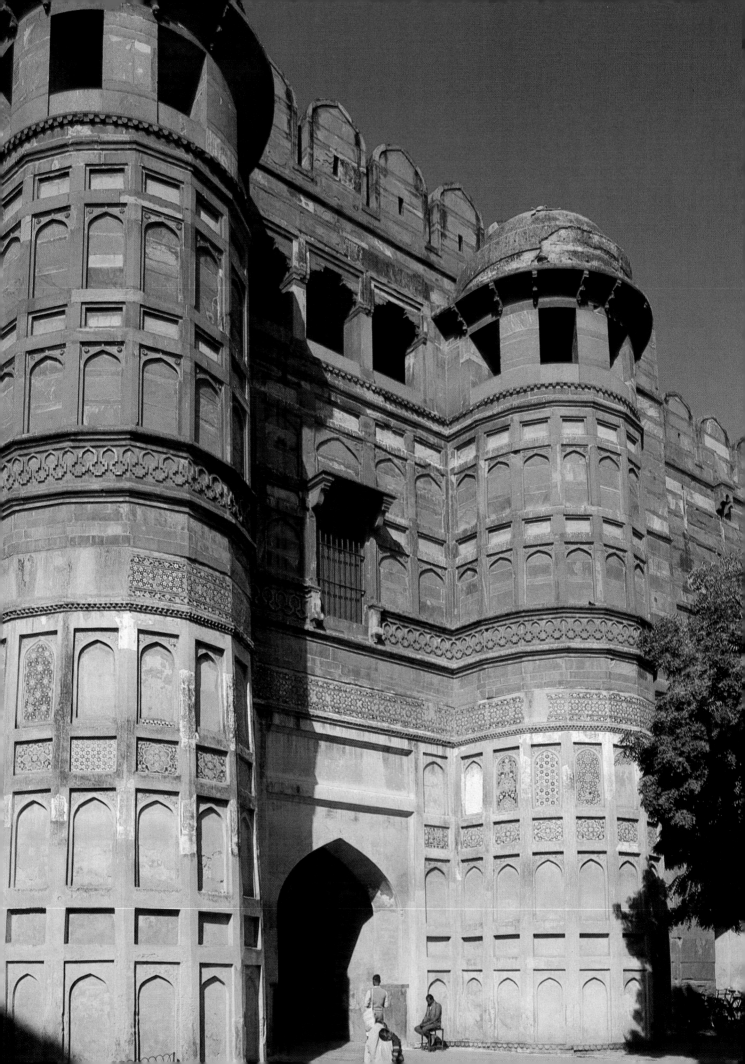

Above and right
The marble buildings within the fort were added by Shah Jahan. Ironically it was within one of these that Shah Jahan spent his last years after his youngest son and successor, the reigning Emperor Aurangzeb, had ordered his arrest.

Left
Agra Fort, which lies on a bend of the Yamuna River, was built by the Emperor Akbar between 1565 and 1574. Its imposing walls of red sandstone and its gateways are decorated with coloured tiles echoing the traditions of Central Asia. It was Akbar's great endeavour to synthesize the two great traditions of Islam and Hinduism and this is reflected in both his politics and architecture.

Eight kilometres (five miles) north of Agra at Sikandra is the tomb of Akbar, started within his lifetime and completed by his son Jahangir in 1613. It has an imposing sandstone gateway with marble inlay work. The tomb in elevation is pyramidical and consists of three storeys. On top is an open courtyard surrounded by a marble screen enclosing the tomb itself. This building is unique in its departure from Islamic architectural tradition, for it has no domed roof.

Above
The exquisite tomb of Itimad-ud-Daulah on the left bank of the Yamuna River was built by Nur Jahan in memory of her father. This small but elegant structure is built entirely in white marble, a feature that appeared for the first time and was an inspiration for the Taj Mahal. The pietra dura *or stone inlay work is of the highest quality, especially in the blend of the colours of the semi-precious stones.*

Right
The gateway to Akbar's tomb at Sikandra is perhaps its most imposing element.

Under the Mughals, Agra developed into an important centre of crafts, specializing in the making of jewellery, marble inlay and stoneware. Thousands of artisans from all of Asia were brought to Agra to help in the building of its magnificent monuments. The traditions still continue today and several areas of the city are inhabited by the descendants of the original craftsmen.

Many of the houses along Agra's back
streets feature traditional doorways such as
these (above), while other buildings display
more modern themes (right).

It is the everyday experience of India that has inspired the visitor and since time immemorial beckoned and held the traveller in its passionate embrace. With its various races and religions comes a multitude of customs and traditions, of art and architecture, smells and sounds that combine to make India the great mosaic it is.

Right
The wonderful street food, tempting as it may look, is best avoided by the novice.

The famous capital city built by Emperor Akbar around 1570 was called Fatehpur Sikri — City of Victory. The village Sikri was associated with a Muslim saint called Shaikh Salim Chishti who foretold the birth of a son and heir to the emperor. When two sons were born, Akbar built the city in thanks. The court later abandoned the city due to the drying up of the water sources. All the palaces and rooms within the royal city continue the distinguishing features of red sandstone, delicate sculptured relief panels and Hindu architectural aspects such as wide hanging eaves and the flat-roofed structures of Akbar's era.

The tomb of Salim Chishti is surrounded by marble, geometrical latticework screens; the canopy above is inlaid with mother-of-pearl. Both Hindus and Muslims pray to the saint for the fulfillment of their wishes. The Buland Darwaza (Gate of Magnificence), which towers above the courtyard of the mosque, was built by Akbar probably following his victory in battle in 1573, when Gujarat fell to him.

*The desert-like conditions of Rajasthan
mean that the camel is the most effective
form of transport. The annual camel fair
held at Pushkar is a spectacular fairground
that spreads over the sand dunes.
Thousands attend the fair each year, joining
the excitement and adding to the colour
and fun.*

Travelling on Indian roads can be an experience in itself. Traffic is often held up by herds of cows trying to cross the roads. The cow is sacred to the Hindus, and is never killed. This often leads, however, to huge herds roaming where they will.

Above
The women may turn their heads, but the children stare cheekily at strangers.

Left
The veneration of the cow follows an ancient tradition in which the animal was vital to a large rural population for assistance in the field, for the use of its dung as fuel, and for its milk as a major source of food.

Women balance jugs and bowls
conveniently on their heads (top and left).
The safe homecoming of the cows and the
cowherd at dusk (above) has often been
eulogized in the romantic traditions of
Indian folk songs, poetry and paintings.

*Daily life for women in rural India is
extremely hard. It is they who bear the
major burden of all chores, rising at dawn
to fetch water, and to feed the cattle; they
toil throughout the day in cooking,
cleaning and helping the menfolk in the
tilling of the land. Girls are taught their
household duties at a very young age and
are often married by the time they are
twelve.*

One of the most colourful sights in Rajasthan is the Banjara men and women in their traditional finery. This nomadic gypsy tribe were pedlars who sold goods to remote villages until modern transport forced them out of business. Always colourful and artistic, they are renowned for their folk songs and dances.

Above
*The Jalmahal on Man Sagar Lake looks
like a pleasure palace but was in fact a
giant blind for aristocratic duck-shooting
parties.*

Right
*Jaipur city as seen from the Nahargarh Fort.
It is today the capital of Rajasthan and was
built by Jai Singh II in the early 18th
century. Surrounded by hills which served
as a natural fortification, it is today a
bustling city of over one million people.*

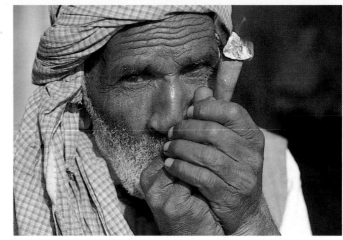

Jaipur is also known as the Pink City, though only a few of its public buildings were built of expensive pink sandstone. The overall pinkness was the idea of Maharaja Ram Singh II who dressed up the rest of the city in the symbolically welcoming colour during the visit of the Prince of Wales in 1876. The Hawa Mahal (above left) affords good and lively views from the top.

The city palace complex in the heart of the old city is divided into a series of courtyards, palaces and gardens. It was started by Jai Singh II but many additions were made by later rulers. The former ruler, Bhawani Singh, still lives in a part of the city palace. The Chandra Mahal, or the Palace of Moons, is at the centre of the complex.

At Gaitor are located the royal cenotaphs or chhatris of the Jaipur royal family. The largest and the most beautiful is the tomb of Jai Singh II (above). Peacocks such as this one (right) roam through the gorgeous gardens of India, occasionally treating a visitor to a magnificent display of feathers.

Following pages
As the golden sunset descends on the Ram Niwas Gardens, India's budding cricketers hurry to finish the game.

The typical traffic of India streams through the three arches of Jaipur's Ajmeri Gate (above). A father squeezes his children onto his bicycle, ready to deliver them to school (right).

The Albert Hall (above left), which now houses the Central Museum in Jaipur, was modelled on the Victoria and Albert Museum in London. Jantar Mantar, or Jai Singh II's observatory, (left), looks at first glance like huge modern sculptures but is in fact a collection of highly complicated astronomical instruments. The solar watch (far left) was accurate to within three seconds. Time was announced to the people of the city by the beating of drums and the firing of cannons.

Following pages
The Amber Fort overlooked by the massive Jaigarh Fort.

Ganesh Pol or Elephant Gate, built in 1640, was Jai Singh I's ceremonial gate. Its latticework windows enabled ladies to watch the processions below without being seen. Over the doorway sits Ganesh the elephant-headed god of learning and good fortune.

Left and below
The roof and walls of the palaces within the fort are profusely decorated with mosaic, fresco and stone sculptures.

Above
An elegant system of paths, trees and shrubberies surrounding a star-shaped pond comprises the roof-garden of the Amber Fort.

Following pages
The sun sets once more over the Taj Mahal.